Mediterranean Cookbook

40 Easy and Delicious Mediterranean Diet Recipes

By

Patrick Smith

ISBN-10: 150033992X
ISBN-13: 978-1500339920

Contents

Section 1: The Diet

The Mediterranean diet is highly popular among health buffs and those trying to lose weight. It is composed of the traditional foods and beverages of the countries surrounding the Mediterranean Sea, including healthy eating and cooking habits such as the following:

- *Making use of good fats* such as extra virgin olive oil, avocados, olives, and sunflower seeds.
- *Reserving the consumption of sweets* during special occasions only.
- *Watching meat size portions.* There are many ways to add a lot of flavor to a dish without the need for an oversized portion of meat. For example, garnish a pasta dish with chopped prosciutto or include tiny strips of sirloin to sautéed vegetables. For main courses, an adequate portion is a maximum of 3.5 ounces (100 grams) of chicken or lean meat.
- *Preparing and eating meals with no meat content* at least once a week.
- *Consuming nutrient-rich eggs and dairy products* throughout the week.
- *Consuming seafood two times a week.* Fish and shellfish such as shrimp, sardines, salmon, herring, and tuna are high in omega-3 fatty acids, which are very beneficial to the health of the brain and heart.
- *Eating breakfast daily.* It is true that breakfast is the most important meal, because what you eat at breakfast will provide most of the energy you need for the whole day. This is why you should include foods that are rich in fiber in your breakfast, such as whole grains and fruits, together with good proteins such as those from dairy products and

eggs. A good breakfast will also help in making you feel full for longer amount of time.

- *Eating lots of vegetables.* Vegetables are the foundation of all meals in the Mediterranean diet.

A substantial amount of scientific research carried out throughout the last six decades show that the Mediterranean diet is one of the world's healthiest ways of eating. Whenever researchers study any single food of the Mediterranean diet, such as extra virgin olive oil, a specific fish, or nut, they discover that its health benefits are linked to the Mediterranean diet as a whole, and cannot be connected to just one specific ingredient.

In other words, there is not a single secret ingredient to good health. Eating an array of whole foods and foods that underwent minimal processing coupled with regular physical activity are the essential concepts of the Mediterranean diet.

The food pyramid shown below illustrates the traditional foods and beverages that, together, make up the balanced and healthy Mediterranean diet. Many of the foods included in this pyramid can also be found in other dietary pyramids. The main difference is in how frequently some of the foods are consumed. Almost any food can be included in a healthy and balanced diet, but the portion size of each food you eat and how often you eat various foods dramatically affect your overall health.

The top of the pyramid includes sweets and red meat. These make up the foods that you should only eat in small amounts. Red meats should not be eaten often and it is better to go for small portions of lean cuts, like flank, T-bone, strip, tenderloin, shoulder, and round. As mentioned earlier, as a main course, the ideal portion size should be 3.5 ounces (100 grams) or less. As for sweets, eat them only as a treat or during special occasions.

The next layer of the pyramid includes eggs, poultry, cheese, and yogurt (dairy products). These make up a focal part of the Mediterranean diet and you should eat them in moderate portion sizes plenty of times per week. For example, you should consume cheese regularly but in small amounts only.

The third layer of the pyramid includes fish and other kinds of seafood. These have their own section because they are chief protein sources. Shellfish like clams, shrimp, oysters, and mussels are high in omega-3 fatty acids, which are extremely beneficial to the heart and brain.

Fish such as sardines, salmon, herring, and tuna have the same benefits. Seafood should be consumed at least two times per week.

The next two layers of the pyramid include herbs, beans, vegetables, fruits, and whole grains. These make up the heart of the Mediterranean diet. Every meal should be based on legumes, spices, herbs, whole grains, vegetables and fruits. Meanwhile, the primary source of dietary fat is extra virgin olive oil, and should be used for almost all baking and cooking, and for dressing vegetables and salads.

All of this needs to go along with exercise. Good exercise is extremely vital for your overall health. This includes laborious workout such as aerobics, running, and jogging, less strenuous activities such as meditation and yoga, and simple physical activity such as walking, household chores, walking back and forth while talking on the phone, and taking the stairs instead of the escalator or elevator.

Also, the Mediterranean diet includes water as its main beverage. Eight to ten glasses of water should be consumed every day. This it is vital for the body to be properly hydrated, it boosts your energy, and it contributes to your overall health and well-being.

In contrast to many diets out there, the Mediterranean diet is not about constricting the amount of food you eat. Instead, it allows you to eat a lot and feel full by preparing and consuming healthy and delectable means with your family and friends as part of your regular way of living. The secret is to prepare meals with whole foods that underwent minimal processing, coupled with regular exercise. The ingredients needed are extremely rich in flavor, offer a lot of health benefits, and are very easy to find.

Health Benefits of the Mediterranean Diet

The Mediterranean diet lifestyle is one of the healthiest diets in the world. In fact, it is one of the most researched and extensively acclaimed diets as proven by a substantial amount of scientific studies conducted over the past sixty years. The following are just some of the amazing health benefits offered by this way of eating:

Numerous studies have shown that following the Mediterranean diet has the following benefits.

1. Improved mental and physical health
2. Improved symptoms of sleep apnea
3. Lower risk for some types of cancer
4. Improvement in bone and teeth health
5. Prevention of Parkinson's disease
6. Slower decline of brain health due to aging, thus lowering the risk of Alzheimer's disease
7. Lower chances of developing depression and similar illnesses in older age
8. Inflammation is reduced and the flowing levels of anti-oxidants are increased
9. Lower risk of developing type 2 diabetes
10. Better management of blood sugar levels in people diagnosed with type 2 diabetes
11. Lower risk of having a heart attack or stroke
12. Lower risk of developing heart diseases
13. The Mediterranean diet in itself tends to induce weight loss, because the portion sizes of certain food types are limited, and the meals are generally savored and enjoyed, not consumed hastily.

The following are some of the numerous highly nutritional foods making up this diet:

Whole grains

These are rich in protein, fiber, and other nutrients. The carbohydrates they contain are the "good" carbohydrates and are a significant choice for a healthy diet. The popular whole grains for the Mediterranean diet include farro, whole wheat couscous, bulgur, brown rice, quinoa, and barley.

Wine

Wine is rich in strong antioxidants coming from grape seeds and skins and has been proven to lower the risk of majority of diseases associated with aging. Low amounts of alcohol improve brain function, while excessive amounts harm the brain and cause fatty liver disease. Men can consume up to two glasses of wine per day, whereas woman should not go beyond one glass per day. For non-wine drinkers, a substitute is 100% organic grape juice.

Seeds and Nuts

Not only do nuts such as walnuts, almonds, hazelnuts, peanuts, pecans, pistachios, and pine nuts, make a good and easy snack, but they are also rich in fiber, protein, and healthy fats that are good for the heart. Seeds are also extremely healthy and go well with roasted vegetables and salads. Good examples include fennel seeds, chia seeds, flax seeds, sunflower seeds and sesame seeds.

Beans

Beans such as white beans, kidney beans, and chickpeas are rich in fiber and protein. They are an excellent substitute for meat and great for vegetarian meals. If you are using canned beans, make sure to drain the liquids and rinse the beans well to wash away the excess sodium.

Yogurt

Yogurt is very high in protein and calcium, which is good for protecting and strengthening bones. It also contains good bacteria that promote healthy digestion. It is recommended to go for Greek yogurt, because it contains twice the amount of protein of regular yogurt, and it also has a nice, tangy flavor.

Tomatoes

These are rich in lycopene and vitamin C. Lycopene is a powerful antioxidant that helps in combating chronic illnesses and promote a healthy immune system.

Fish and seafood

In the Mediterranean diet, fish and seafood should be consumed twice per week. Fish contains a lot of healthy fats. Fish such as mackerel, sardines, tuna, and salmon are high in omega-3 fatty acids, which are beneficial to the health of the heart and brain.

Avocados

These are rich in vitamin E, healthy monounsaturated fats, and fiber. In addition, they are available any time of the year. You can incorporate avocados in salads, use them in dips, or just eat them on their own!

Frequently Asked Questions

The Mediterranean diet uses mainly olive oil and also includes nuts. Aren't these high in fats?

When talking about fats in food, you should know two very important things. First, determine the kind of fat. Second, determine the amount of fat. For example, even healthy fats, if taken in high amounts, can result in weight gain.

Saturated fats are typically found in foods that came from animal sources, such as eggs, dairy products, and meat. Trans fats are artificial and can be found in processed foods. They clog arteries and are a major cause for heart disease. After decades of making people sick, trans fats were finally banned by the American Food and Drug Administration at end of 2013. However, keep in mind that it will take time for this to be implemented for all processed foods out there.

The ideal thing to do is stay away or restrict your intake of trans fats or saturated fats, because these kinds of fats can increase LDL-C (low-density lipoprotein cholesterol) aka "bad" cholesterol, and lower the HDL-C (high-density lipoprotein cholesterol) aka "good" cholesterol.

On the other hand, the fats contained in nuts and olive oil are polyunsaturated fats and monounsaturated fats, which are *healthy* fats that do not increase LDL-C. Then again, do not forget that olive oil and nuts are high in calories too, so you should consume them in reasonable quantities.

An even better example for healthy saturated fats are coconut products. Though not part of the Mediterranean diet, coconut is extremely healthy, and it is advisable to replace butter/margarine with coconut oil.

What are some tips for beginners of the Mediterranean diet?

It is best to make a meal plan for all your meals and snacks for every week in advance. This way, you will know which foods to stock up in your kitchen, and you will be motivated to follow the meals you planned.

Also, always substitute olive oil or coconut oil for meals that call for butter. Never use margarine.

If possible, consider consulting a professional dietitian so you can be guided more accurately in the food choices suitable for your lifestyle and culture.

Why is it called the Mediterranean diet?

This way of eating is characteristic of the countries which surround the Mediterranean Sea, such as Lebanon, Libya, Croatia, Israel, Greece, Albania, Algeria, Turkey, Tunisia, Malta, Syria, Morocco, Egypt, Italy, France, and Spain.

Will I always feel hungry once I start following the Mediterranean diet?

No. The Mediterranean diet is not a diet wherein you will starve yourself. Rather, it is a lifestyle. It involves eating whole grains, nuts, beans, fish, vegetables fruits, and meat in proper proportions and frequency, coupled with regular physical activity. As long as you follow the diet properly, you can still get to eat a lot and feel full longer while staying healthy and maintaining or losing your weight.

Is it easy to follow the Mediterranean Diet correctly?

Yes, because you do not count calories, but simply eat good foods. The food choices are diverse and have a great taste. Here are some tips for this diet:

Consume small portions of cheese and yogurt every day. For example, feta cheese makes a great ingredient for salads, which means that even a salad can be a vessel for your daily cheese intake.

Go for lean meat such as chicken, turkey, fish, and beans as your source of protein. You can enjoy red meat during special occasions.

Consume sweets during special occasions or as a treat.

Base your every meal on whole grains, vegetables, fruits, nuts, beans, spices, and herbs.

Go for healthy fats such as those found in fish like tuna, salmon, sardines, and mackerel, avocados, nuts, extra virgin olive oil, and extra virgin coconut oil.

Why should I abide by the Mediterranean diet?

Studies conducted over the last six decades have shown that the Mediterranean diet is one of the healthiest diets in the world. In addition, it offers diverse food choices that are rich in flavor.

Is it true that the Mediterranean diet is just another fad diet?

No, the Mediterranean diet is a lifestyle. It is a way of eating that is sustainable and has been shown to improve health and lower the risk of chronic illnesses.

Is it true that the Mediterranean diet is a new way of eating?

No, the Mediterranean diet started in the 1940s. Back then, a researcher named Ancel Keys discovered that most of the people in Mediterranean countries had very low rates of heart disease and were living longer lives than people in the northern part of Europe.

Does the Mediterranean diet involve foods that are foreign and hard to access?

No. Almost every food included in the Mediterranean diet pyramid can be found in your local grocery store. In fact, all you need are vegetables, fruits, whole grains, dairy products, fish, nuts, and olive oil. The next chapter will show you which foods you should stock up in your kitchen so you can easily prepare a Mediterranean meal at any time.

May I consume sweets or meats if I follow this diet?

Red meats and sweets can be consumed during special occasions or just occasionally. Lean meat such as chicken, turkey, and fish are recommended to be eaten more often.

Is it true that I will lose weight if I follow this diet?

The Mediterranean diet is not necessarily a way of eating intended to make you lose weight, but weight loss is one of its added benefits if it is followed properly. This is because the Mediterranean diet involves eating healthy meals in proper portions coupled with regular physical activity.

You are most likely to reach and maintain your own normal weight, not going above or below that. There is a certain weight that your brain considers normal for your body, something that is different for every one of us. If you eat too much and do not have an eating disorder, your brain will try to regulate your metabolism and hunger to bring your weight back down. If you eat too little, like in most diets, your brain will believe there is a famine and you are starving. It will do all it can to get you back to normal levels: this is why most diets do not work and people end up with more weight than before.

Being healthy is not about being slim, it is about keeping what your brain considers to be the normal weight for your body.

With the Mediterranean diet, you give your body exactly what it really wants: healthy foods in enough quantity.

What Should Be in Your Kitchen

In your pantry

Vinegars: white wine vinegar, red wine vinegar, fig vinegar, apple cider vinegar, champagne vinegar, balsamic vinegar, vinaigrette

Canned tomatoes: sun-dried tomatoes, diced tomatoes, tomato sauce, tomato paste

Seeds: sunflower seeds, sesame seeds, flax seeds, fennel seeds

Salt: table salt, sea salt, kosher salt

Red wine

Potatoes (all kinds)

Pastas (all kinds, including whole grain pasta)

Olives (black olives, Kalamata olives)

Nuts: walnuts, pistachios, pine nuts, peanuts, hazelnuts, pecans, almonds

Raw honey

Herbs and spices: Italian seasoning, dried oregano, dried basil, turmeric powder, cumin seeds, ground cinnamon, garlic powder, onion powder, curry powder, dill, rosemary, thyme, parsley, black pepper, bay leaves, fresh garlic, fresh onions, coriander, sage, saffron, parsley, mint, ground black pepper, crushed red peppers, chili flakes, cayenne pepper, paprika, ginger

Grains: quinoa, rice, polenta, oats, millet, farro, couscous

Dried fruits: prunes, raisins, figs dates, cranberries, cherries, blueberries, raspberries, apricots

Crackers: whole-wheat/whole-grain crackers that contain two to three grams of fiber per serving

Oatmeal and cereals

Capers: They will last for up to six months in the refrigerator.

Canned seafood: tuna, sardines, salmon, clams, anchovies

Breads: pita, focaccia, bread crumbs, and other whole grain or whole wheat breads.

Beans: lentils, kidney beans, white beans, fava, cannellini, and chickpeas.

In your freezer

Gelato

Sorbet

Frozen chicken stock

Frozen vegetables

Frozen seafood

Frozen meat and poultry

Frozen fruits

Yogurt

Sparkling wine and white wine

Vegetables

Tapenade

Pickles

Pesto

Mustard

Fruits: grapes, berries, mangoes

Eggs

Cheese (hard and soft varieties): feta cheese, Parmesan, mozzarella, goat cheese

On your counter

Extra virgin olive oil. You can also use coconut oil, due to its immense health benefits.

Fresh tomatoes: plum tomatoes, cherry tomatoes, grape tomatoes, Roma tomatoes

Fresh fruits: tangerines, pomegranates, pears, peaches, apples, plums, bananas, dates, nectarines, melons, oranges, limes, lemons, grapefruit, figs, clementines, cherries, apricots, and avocados. These fruits are best stored at room temperature.

Section 2: Recipes

Breakfast Recipes

1. Vegetarian Omelet

In the Mediterranean countries, eggs are eaten often and make a good choice for breakfast, because they offer a lot of vitamins, minerals, and protein. Though eggs contain high levels of cholesterol, consuming eggs in moderation does not have any established harmful effects on cardiovascular health. This recipe is for a simple Mediterranean vegetarian omelet that is easy to make, yet healthy and delicious!

Ingredients

2 tbs fresh **parsley leaves** (chopped)
½ cup **goat cheese** (crumbled)
6 **eggs**
¼ cup **artichoke hearts**
¼ green **olives** (pitted, chopped)
1 **Roma tomato** (diced)
2 cups fresh bulbs of **fennel** (sliced thinly)
1 tbs extra virgin **olive oil**
¼ tsp **table salt**
½ tsp **black pepper** (ground)

Makes: 4 servings
Calories: 132 per serving

Instructions

Marinate the artichoke hearts in water for a few minutes, then rinse and drain thoroughly. Chop into small pieces and set aside.

Wash the fresh parsley leaves and rinse thoroughly. Set aside 2 tbs of the chopped parsley leaves.

Slice the fennel bulbs into thin slices, then set aside.

Preheat the oven to 325 F (160 °C).

In a large skillet, heat the extra virgin olive oil. Once hot, sauté the sliced fennel for about 5 minutes, or until tender.

Add in the chopped artichoke hearts, pitted olives, and diced tomato and sauté for an additional 3 minutes, or until soft.

In a large bowl, whisk the eggs. Add the table salt and freshly ground black pepper and whisk again until the seasonings are well distributed.

Pour the egg mixture into the skillet containing the sautéed vegetables and stir using a wooden spoon for 2 minutes. Transfer the omelet to a baking tray.

Crumble the goat cheese over the omelet and bake in the oven for about 5 minutes, or until the eggs are cooked through and the cheese has melted.

Garnish with chopped parsley leaves on top. Serve immediately.

2. Breakfast Egg Wraps

This is a simple dish of scrambled eggs with feta cheese covered in tortilla wraps. It has a light, salty and tangy flavor thanks to the feta cheese, which complements the eggs perfectly.

Ingredients

Tortilla wraps
2 tbs **spring onions** (minced)
2 tbs **red peppers** (roasted)
¾ cup **feta cheese** (crumbled)
½ tsp **dried oregano**
½ tsp **dried basil**
¼ tsp **garlic powder**
¼ tsp **salt** and **black pepper** (ground)
¼ cup **light sour cream**
6 **eggs**
1 tsp extra virgin **olive oil**

Makes: 4 servings
Calories: 245 per serving

Instructions

Chop the red peppers into small pieces, then sauté in a skillet for a few minutes. Set aside.

Chop the spring onions and set aside.

In a large mixing bowl, put in the eggs and whisk well.

Add in the garlic powder, dried oregano, dried basil, black pepper, table salt, and sour cream. Whisk together until well combined.

Add in the feta cheese.

Heat the extra virgin olive oil in a skillet. Once hot, pour in the egg mixture and cook until most of the eggs are cooked but overall still slightly wet. Add in the chopped spring onions and the red peppers. Stir well until everything has been cooked completely.

If you want, you can garnish the top with additional feta cheese.

Wrap the scrambled eggs in tortilla wraps and serve immediately.

3. Cheese and Zucchini Frittata

In the Mediterranean countries, people usually use frittatas and scrambled eggs to use up leftovers, which is a good idea so nothing will go to waste. Aside from saving you money, it is also an excellent way to add some extra vegetables to your meal.

Ingredients

2 oz. (60 g) **goat cheese** or **feta cheese** (crumbled)
1 **garlic clove** (crushed, minced)
1 tbs extra virgin **olive oil**
1/8 tsp **black pepper** (ground)
¼ tsp **table salt**
2 tbs **skim milk**
8 **eggs**
2 medium-sized **zucchinis**

Makes: 4 servings
Calories: 127 per serving

Instructions

Cut the zucchinis into slices. Set aside.

Peel and crush the garlic clove. Mince it finely. Set aside.

In a large mixing bowl, whisk the eggs. Add in the ground black pepper, table salt, and skim milk. Whisk again until thoroughly combined. Set aside.

In a large skillet, put in the extra virgin olive oil and heat over medium heat. Once the oil is hot, add in the minced garlic and cook for about half a minute while constantly stirring to prevent it from burning. Then, add the slices of zucchini and continue cooking for about five more minutes.

While the zucchini is being cooked, preheat the oven to 350°F (180°C).

Pour the egg mixture onto the zucchini and garlic mixture and stir well for about one minute or until the eggs have reached your desired level of doneness. Transfer the mixture to a circular baking pan. Crumble the goat cheese or feta cheese on top.

Bake in the preheated oven for about 10 to 12 minutes, or until the eggs are fully cooked.

Once done, immediately remove the baking pan from the oven and let it sit for 3 minutes.

Remove the frittata from the baking pan and transfer to a chopping board or a clean wooden surface. Slice the frittata into four equal portions.

You can serve the frittatas immediately or allow it to cool to room temperature before serving.

4. Breakfast Smoothie

Nothing beats a delicious and refreshing smoothie, especially in summer. Not only is it delicious, but also extremely healthy! This recipe is for a traditional Mediterranean breakfast smoothie, but it is good for any time of the day.

Ingredients

4 **ice cubes**
½ cup **skim milk**
½ cup **beet juice**
1 small **ripe mango**
1 frozen **banana** (sliced)
½-inch (1.3 cm) fresh **ginger root**
2 cups **organic baby spinach**

Makes: 2 servings
Calories: 162 per serving

Instructions

Peel the fresh ginger root and slice into thin strips. Set aside. Cut the frozen banana into thin slices. Set aside.

Cut the ripe mango into three parts and remove the middle part (containing the seed). Peel off the skin and cut the mango into cubes. Set aside.

Prepare the beet juice. If you prefer, you can purchase canned beets at the grocery store that already includes beet juice. However, it is best to make your own beet juice by adding the beets to a juicer.

Once you have the beet juice ready, transfer it to a blender together with other ingredients. Blend until smooth.

5. Quinoa Meal

This recipe is for quinoa with a cinnamon and nutty flavor, made even healthier and more delicious by the addition of honey, toasted almonds, apricots, and dates.

Ingredients

5 dried **apricots**
2 pitted **dates**
2 tbs raw **honey**
1 tsp **vanilla extract**
1 tsp **sea salt**
2 cups **skim milk**
1 cup **quinoa**
1 tsp **cinnamon** (ground)
¼ cup raw **almonds**

Makes: 4 servings
Calories: 310 per serving

Instructions

Chop the dried apricots, pitted dates and raw almonds into small pieces and set aside.

Heat a skillet over medium heat. Once hot, put in the raw almonds and roast them for 3 to 5 minutes, or until they are golden in color. Set aside.

Heat a large saucepan over medium heat. Put in the quinoa and the ground cinnamon and mix well. Allow them to be heated through. Once done, add in the sea salt and skim milk, then mix well. Increase the heat and let the mixture boil.

Once boiling, reduce to a simmer. Put the lid on and simmer for about fifteen minutes.

Add in the apricots, dates, raw honey, vanilla extract, and half of the roasted almonds. Mix well. Serve immediately in 4 individual bowls.

Top each serving with the remaining toasted almonds.

6. Potatoes with Bacon and Scrambled Eggs

This recipe combines many good ingredients to a wholesome and delicious breakfast meal.

Ingredients

¼ cup **feta cheese** (crumbled)
3 cups **potatoes** (roasted, diced)
2 cups fresh **baby spinach leaves**
¼ cup **kalamata olives**, pitted and chopped
8 strips **bacon** (cooked, crumbled)
1 tbs **extra virgin olive oil**
8 **eggs**
2 tbs **milk**
½ tsp **kosher salt**
¼ tsp **black pepper** (ground)
3 tbs **red peppers** (chopped, roasted)
Seasoning (vegetable broth, garlic salt, pepper, and paprika)

Makes: 4 servings
Calories: 145 per serving

Instructions

Preheat the oven to 375 F (190°C).

Quarter the potatoes and place them in bowl. For the seasoning, add enough vegetable broth to thoroughly wet the potatoes. Also season with garlic salt, ground pepper and paprika to taste.

Place the potato quarters on a baking sheet and bake for 25 - 30 minutes, or until tender.

Heat olive oil in a skillet over medium heat, then add spinach leaves and cook until wilted. Remove and set aside.

Spray another skillet with cooking spray. Combine salt, pepper, milk and eggs in a bowl. Stir to combine, then add the mixture to the skillet over medium heat. Scramble the eggs using a spoon or spatula, then add the feta cheese, spinach, olives, bacon, and red peppers. Stir to combine.

Place potatoes in a serving bowl and top with the scrambled eggs and bacon. Serve immediately.

7. Mediterranean Yoghurt

Yoghurt recipes are not only delicious and a treat, they are healthy and make for a nutritious breakfast. You can use any kind of fresh berries for this recipe that you want. My recommendation is blueberries, blackberries, or strawberries.

Ingredients

¼ cup organic **honey**
4 cups plain **Greek yogurt**
2 cups fresh **berries** of your choice
1 cup uncooked **grano**
¼ cup organic **honey**
¼ tsp **kosher salt**

Makes: 8 servings
Calories: 225 per serving

Instructions

Prepare the grano on the evening before serving by soaking it in 6 cups of water overnight.

In the morning, drain the grano, place it in a saucepan, add 6 cups of water and set heat to high. Once boiling, reduce heat and simmer for 25 minutes, or until the grano is tender.

Remove from heat and drain. Stir in honey and salt, then allow it to cool. Place ¼ cup of the Greek yoghurt in a serving glass, preferably a parfait glass. Add 3 tbs of grano and 2 tbs of your chosen berries to the yoghurt. Continue making layers until the glass is full, then repeat with another glass.

There should be enough material to prepare 8 glasses. Alternatively, you can make 1 glass bowl of yoghurt and layers.

8. Sweet Breakfast Muesli

This Mediterranean muesli is quick and very easy to make. It is delicious and healthy. If you prefer it less sweet, take less honey.

Ingredients

3 tbs **pitted dates** (chopped)
3 tbs dried **apricots** (chopped)
3 tbs dried **figs** (chopped)
1/3 cup **honey**
¼ cup **oat bran**
1 cup **oats**
1 cup low-fat **milk**
1 cup plain **yogurt**
½ cup **walnuts** (chopped)
Fresh **berries** of your choice (optional)

Makes: 5 servings
Calories: 265 per serving

Instructions

Simply combine all of the ingredients in a bowl and mix together.

For maximum taste, especially on hot days, chill for 2 hours before serving.

If desired, garnish with berries of your choice.

9. Fruit and Nut Breakfast

This muesli recipe comes from Italy. It is light, yet very nutritious, combining fruits, almonds and sunflower seeds.

Ingredients

1 tsp **almonds**, (sliced)
¼ **mango**, (peeled, diced)
1 tsp **sunflower** seeds
½ **apple**, (cored, peeled, diced)
½ cup **oats**
1 cup low fat **milk**

Makes: 3 servings
Calories: 115 per serving

Instructions

Combine the milk and oats in a bowl.

Microwave on high a setting for 2 minutes.

Remove and stir in the sunflower seeds and almond, then top with diced apple and mango.

10. Salmon Omelet

Salmon is a common Mediterranean ingredient. This recipe combines it with asparagus to accompany a delicious omelet.

Ingredients

2 **asparagus spears**
2 **eggs**
½ tsp **extra virgin olive oil**
4 oz. (115 g) **salmon**
1 tsp low fat **milk**
2 tbs **onion** (diced)
¼ tsp **lemon juice**
½ tbs **parsley**
Sea Salt, ground **pepper**, **chives,** and **dill** to taste

Makes: 2 servings
Calories: 145 per serving

Instructions

Heat the olive oil in a skillet over medium heat. Add the diced onion and sauté for 3 minutes, or until translucent. Add the lemon juice and asparagus, then sauté for another 2 minutes.

Combine the milk, parsley, and eggs in a bowl and beat the mixture. Season with sea salt, ground pepper, chives, and dill.

Add the mixture and salmon to the skillet. Reduce heat to low and cook for 3-5 minutes.

Fold the omelet in half, then cook for 1 more minute.

Lunch Recipes

1. Classic Chicken Salad

This salad includes a generous amount of chicken, red onion marinated in red wine vinegar, capers, olives, and extra virgin olive oil. You can eat it as is, or serve it in lettuce cups.

Ingredients

4 tbs **parsley leaves** (chopped)
1 tbs **basil leaves** (chopped)
1 tbs **oregano leaves** (chopped)
1 tsp **chili flakes**
1 ½ cups **olives** (pitted, chopped)
2 tbs **capers**
4 tbs **extra virgin olive oil**
2 lbs. (900 g) skinless, boneless **chicken breasts** (shredded)
4 tbs **red wine vinegar**
1 cup **red onions** (chopped)
Salt and **black pepper** (ground)

Makes: 8 servings
Calories: 125 per serving

Instructions

Rinse the chicken breasts (make sure they are skinless and boneless) well and pat dry with paper towels. Shred into small pieces. Set aside.

In a medium-sized bowl, combine chopped onions with the red wine vinegar. Stir well and set aside to allow the red onions to absorb the vinegar's flavor.

Meanwhile, put enough water and a bit of salt in a large saucepan and bring it to a boil. Slice the chicken breasts in half. Transfer them to the saucepan once the water has started boiling. Reduce to very low heat and allow the chicken breasts to simmer for 10 to 15 minutes, until fully cooked.

While the chicken is simmering, combine the chopped oregano leaves, basil leaves, chili flakes, olives, capers, and extra virgin olive oil in a large bowl. Stir well until thoroughly combined. Set aside.

When the chicken is cooked, transfer on a chopping board and allow it to cool. Meanwhile, add in the marinated red onions to the bowl containing the oregano and olives. Mix well.

When the chicken is cool enough, cut it into shreds, then add into the olive mixture. Stir well to combine.

Add the chopped parsley into the chicken and olive mixture, then stir again until well combined. Season with table salt and freshly ground black pepper.

Serve immediately, or let it cool to room temperature before serving.

2. Classic Mediterranean Pizza

This pizza recipe features classic Mediterranean flavors like olives, feta cheese, oregano, zucchini, and tomatoes. It is a great, healthy alternative to traditional pizzas but just as delicious.

Ingredients

½ cup pitted **black olives** (chopped)
8 oz. (230 g) **feta cheese** (crumbled)
½ tsp dried **oregano** or 2 tbs **oregano leaves** (chopped)
1 **zucchini** (sliced thinly)
14.5 oz. (410 g) canned **tomatoes** (diced)
1 lb. (450 g) **pizza dough** (frozen)
2 tbs extra virgin **olive oil**

Makes: 8 servings
Calories: 270 per serving

Instructions

Trim the ends of the zucchini, then cut it in half lengthwise. Cut into thin slices. Set aside.

Drain the diced tomatoes and set aside.

Preheat the oven to 475F (250°C). Use 1 tbs of extra virgin olive oil to grease the bottom and sides of a baking pan.

Transfer the pizza dough (thawed) to the baking pan, roll it out and evenly spread it across the pan. If the pizza dough is too firm at first, let it stand for a couple of minutes before proceeding.

Add in the diced tomatoes and spread across the pizza dough.

Arrange the slices of zucchini on top of the diced tomatoes. Top the zucchini slices with the dried oregano or chopped fresh oregano leaves.

Crumble the feta cheese on top of the pizza. Add in the pitted olives last and spread evenly across the pizza.

Bake the pizza in the preheated oven for 15 to 20 minutes, or until the cheese is browned lightly, and the crust has become golden brown (you can use a spatula to lift up the pizza to check the crust).

Remove the pizza from the oven and drizzle the remaining 1 tbs extra virgin olive oil evenly across the top.

Let the pizza rest for 5 minutes before cutting and serving.

3. Mediterranean Potato Pancakes

Potato pancakes are traditionally eaten during the Hanukkah, a Jewish holiday, but a lot of people eat them any time of the year because they really have a year-round appeal. This recipe for potato pancakes is made more exciting with the inclusion of flour made from chickpeas, and a lot of spices and herbs.

Ingredients

½ tsp **turmeric powder** or **turmeric** (ground)
1 ½ tsp **cumin seeds**
3 tbs extra virgin **olive oil**
¼ tsp **cayenne pepper**
½ tsp **black pepper** (ground)
1 ½ tsp **table salt**
2 tsp **coriander** (ground)
1 ½ tbs **jalapeño** (seeds removed, minced)
2 large **eggs**
½ cup **chickpea flour**
½ cup **cilantro leaves** (chopped)
½ cup **spring onions** (finely chopped)
1 large **white onion** (grated)
2 ½ lbs. (1,15 kg) **white potatoes** (grated)

Makes: 18 servings
Calories: 83 per serving

Instructions

Peel the potatoes and grate them. Transfer to a large enough bowl and pour in enough cold water to submerge the potatoes. Set aside.

Beat the eggs in a small bowl and set aside.

Transfer the grated onion and grated potatoes in a large colander and drain thoroughly. Mix them well. Then, using your bare hands, squeeze the potato and onion mixture to wheedle out as much liquids as possible.

Transfer the potato and onion mixture to a large mixing bowl. Add in the chopped spring onions and stir well.

Add in the cayenne pepper, ground black pepper, table salt, ground coriander, minced jalapeño, beaten eggs, chickpea flour, and chopped cilantro leaves. Stir everything together until well combined.

In a large skillet, heat 2 tbs extra virgin olive oil. Add in the turmeric powder and cumin seeds and sauté for about 30 seconds, stirring constantly. Transfer the turmeric and cumin mixture into the potato mixture. Cover with a lid and let the flavors infuse for about 30 minutes.

Meanwhile, preheat the oven to 250F (120°C). Heat the remaining 1 tbs of extra virgin olive oil in the same skillet you used for the turmeric and cumin seeds. Add 3 tbs of the infused potato mixture to the skillet for each potato pancake and flatten it to roughly 4-inch (10 cm) rounds using a spatula. Cook for 5 minutes per side, or until golden.

Transfer the potato pancakes to a baking dish and keep them warm in the oven. Continue cooking the potato pancakes in the skillet, adding more extra virgin olive oil if needed.

Serve the potato pancakes immediately.

4. Greek Shrimp Pasta

Shrimp pasta is a very quick meal to prepare. Aside from that, it is colorful, fresh, and very flavorful. You can use any type of pasta you want for it.

Ingredients

¼ cup **feta cheese**
8 oz. (225 g) uncooked **pasta**
¼ tsp **black pepper** (ground)
2 tbs drained **capers**
1/3 cup pitted **Kalamata olives** (chopped)
¼ **fresh basil leaves** (chopped)
2 cups **plum tomatoes** (diced)
1 lb. (450 g) **shrimp** (peeled)
2 **cloves of garlic** (crushed, minced)
3 tsp **extra virgin olive oil**

Makes: 4 servings
Calories: 204 per serving

Instructions

Peel off the shells of the shrimp. Set aside.

Rinse the fresh basil leaves and drain well. Chop into thin slices. Set aside.

Finely chop the pitted Kalamata olives. Set aside.

Peel the garlic cloves and crush them. Then, mince finely and set aside.

Dice the plum tomatoes and set aside.

Fill a large saucepan with enough water and a bit of salt, and bring to a boil.

Once boiling, put in the uncooked pasta and cook according to package directions until *al dente*. Drain the pasta well and put back into the saucepan. Set aside.

In a large skillet, put in the extra virgin olive oil and heat it. Once the oil is hot, add in the minced garlic and cook for about 30 seconds while stirring.

Add in the shrimp and sauté for one more minute.

Add in the chopped basil leaves and the diced plum tomatoes. Reduce to low heat and allow to simmer for 3 minutes, or until the tomatoes are soft.

Add in the black pepper, capers, and Kalamata olives. Stir well to combine.

Transfer the shrimp mixture to the saucepan containing the cooked pasta. Toss everything together until thoroughly combined.

Divide the shrimp pasta equally between four individual serving bowls. Top with crumbled feta cheese on top.

Serve immediately.

5. Mediterranean Pita Bread with Hummus

Hummus is a classic Middle Eastern delicacy that is usually used as a dip and served with pita bread. It is made from pureed chickpeas and tahini, a special kind of sesame paste. This recipe is very easy to prepare and great for the Mediterranean diet!

Ingredients

4 **pepperoncini peppers** (sliced thinly)
2 large **plum tomatoes** (sliced thinly)
2 small **cucumbers** (sliced thinly)
4 tbs **feta cheese** (crumbled)
4 6-inch (15 cm) whole-wheat round **pita bread**
1 cup **hummus** with **roasted peppers**

Makes: 4 servings
Calories: 310 per serving

Instructions

Cut the pita bread rounds in half.

Spread 2 tbs of hummus on each pit bread half.

Crumble feta cheese equally between the 8 pita bread halves.

Arrange the slices of tomatoes and cucumbers on top of the pita bread halves.

Lastly, top with slices of pepperoncini peppers.

Serve immediately and enjoy!

6. Pasta Coconut Salad

As mentioned in section 1, coconut products are extremely healthy and make a great addition to the Mediterranean diet. This recipe makes use of this ingredient. It can either be seen as a meal or noodle salad, depending on whether you let it cool at the end or eat it warm.

Ingredients

4 tbs **coconut oil**
2-3 cloves **garlic**, minced
Shredded **coconut**
½ cup **red onion** (diced)
¼ cup **yellow bell pepper** (diced)
¼ cup **green bell pepper** (diced)
¼ cup **red bell pepper** (diced)
1 lb. **penne pasta** (cooked)
¼ cup **sun dried tomatoes** in **olive oil** (chopped)
½ cup **basil** (chopped)
Salt and **pepper** (optional)
Parmesan cheese (grated, optional)

Makes: 4 servings
Calories: 255 per serving

Instructions

Make sure you have the pasta cooked by the end, so either cook it first or get it done at the same time.

Melt the coconut oil in a medium sized frying pan. Combine garlic, onion, all peppers, and basil in the pan, then stir them together. Cook until tender.

Transfer the mix from the pan to the cooked pasta. Add the sun dried tomatoes and stir.

Optionally, season with salt and pepper and top with parmesan cheese.

Finally, top with shredded coconut.

For salad, let it cool down and chill it in the fridge. For a meal, serve it hot.

7. Stuffed Bell Peppers

Recipes of this kind are interesting, delicious and nutritious at the same time. Peppers are the perfect vessels to combine many ingredients.

Ingredients

3 **red bell peppers**
1 lb. (450 g) **lean beef** (ground)
1 **egg** (lightly beaten)
28 oz. (800 g) low-sodium stewed **tomatoes** (chopped)
1/3 cup **feta cheese** (crumbled)
10 oz. (280 g) frozen **spinach**
½ cup **bulgur**
1 medium **zucchini**, (coarsely grated)
1 small **onion** (minced)
½tsp dried **oregano**
½ tsp **salt** and
¼ tsp **black pepper** (ground)

Makes: 6 servings
Calories: 225 per serving

Instructions

Preheat the oven to 350F (180°C) Combine the spinach, onion, zucchini, beef, bulgur, oregano, salt, black pepper, and egg in a bowl.

Cut the bell peppers in half lengthwise, then remove the cores and ribs. Place the halves on a baking dish and fill with the mixture from the bowl. Add the chopped tomatoes to the bell peppers and top with feta cheese.

Cover with foil and bake for 35 minutes. Uncover and continue cooking for another 20 minutes, until the peppers are tender.

8. Tomato Soup

This is my standard recipe for tomato soup. It is perfect for lunch or as entry for dinner and has a great taste whether it is served hot or cold.

Ingredients

28 oz. (800 g) **tomatoes** (cored)
½ **onion**, (chopped)
2 cups **vegetable broth**
½ cup **white wine**
2 tbs **tomato paste**
2 tsp **dried basil**
½ tsp **cumin** (ground)
2/3 cup low fat **milk**
1 tsp **salt**
¼ tsp **black pepper** (ground)

Makes 5 servings
Calories: 150 per serving

Instructions

Place all ingredients except the milk in a slow cooker. Cover, set to low heat and cook for 4 hours.

Remove and add to a blender. Let it cool for 30 minutes. When cooled, blend completely.

Pour into a saucepan and add the milk. Heat it up, but don't boil it.

Optionally, serve with crackers or croutons.

9. Mediterranean Lamb Pilaf

This is my standard recipe for tomato soup. It is perfect for lunch or as entry for dinner and has a great taste whether it is served hot or cold.

Ingredients

¾ lb. (340 g) lean **lamb** (ground)
1 large **onion** (chopped)
14 oz. (400 g) fat-free **chicken broth**
1 **plum tomato** (chopped)
3 **garlic** cloves (minced)
1 **carrot** (chopped)
1 cup uncooked **rice**
2 tbs **mint** (chopped)
3 tbs **lemon juice**
¼ tsp **cinnamon** (ground)
¼ cup **flat-leaf parsley** (chopped, divided)
¾ tsp **salt**

Makes 4 servings
Calories: 375 per serving

Instructions

Place the onion, garlic, carrot and lamb in a skillet over medium heat. Cook for 5 minutes while stirring to crumble the meat.

Add the cinnamon and rice, stir and sauté for 3 minutes. Add the chicken broth, then bring to a boil. Cover, reduce the heat and simmer for 25 minutes, or until all liquid is absorbed.

Remove from heat and add the tomato, parsley, salt, mint and lemon juice. Stir to mix, cover and let it sit for 5 minutes.

10. Ratatouille

Ratatouille is a delicious vegetable stew that originated in France. This version is prepared in a frying pan and works very well with pasta.

Ingredients

1 lb. (450 g) **bell peppers**, (stemmed, seeded, diced)
28 oz. (800 g) **tomatoes** (diced)
8 oz. (225 g) **eggplant** (diced)
8 oz. (225 g) **zucchini** (diced)
8 oz. (225 g) **yellow summer squash** (diced)
8 oz. (225 g) **onion** (peeled, diced)
3 tbs **extra virgin olive oil**
2 **garlic** cloves (peeled, minced)
¾ cup **basil leaves** (chopped)
½ tsp **salt**
¼ tsp **pepper**

Makes 4 servings
Calories: 220 per serving

Instructions

Heat 1 ½ tbs olive oil in a frying pan over medium heat. Add garlic and onion, then sauté for 5 minutes while stirring, until onion is translucent.

Add the eggplant, salt, tomatoes, pepper, and ½ cup water to the pan. Cover, reduce heat and simmer for 10 minutes, or until the eggplant is soft. Keep stirring occasionally.

Add the bell peppers, yellow squash, and zucchini. Cover and cook for another 10 minutes, or until the squash is tender.

Add the remaining 1 ½ tbs olive oil and basil. Serve and enjoy!

Snack Recipes

1. Marinated Feta Cheese and Olives

Feta cheese and olives marinated with garlic, lemon, and rosemary are amazing together with warm crusty bread slices.

Ingredients

1 **warm crusty bread** such as baguette (sliced)
½ tsp **black pepper** (ground)
1 pinch of **red peppers** (crushed)
1 tsp **fresh rosemary leaves** (chopped)
2 **garlic cloves** (minced finely)
Juice of ½ **lemon**
Zest of ½ **lemon**
Grated rind of 1 lemon
2 tbs extra virgin **olive oil**
½ cup **feta cheese** (diced)
1 cup pitted **Kalamata olives** (sliced)

Makes: 2 servings
Calories: 102 per serving

Instructions

In a large mixing bowl, combine the freshly ground black pepper, crushed red peppers, chopped rosemary leaves, minced garlic, lemon juice, and lemon zest. Mix well.

Add in the diced feta cheese and the halved pitted Kalamata olives. Stir well until fully combined. Let the flavors infuse for at least 5 minutes.

Serve with the slices of warm crusty bread. You can prepare this ahead of time and refrigerate, covered, for up to 24 hours.

2. Olives and Tomatoes with Cheese Picnic

This recipe combines tangy cheese, salty olives, and sweet tomatoes. It is great as a snack or for picnics and can be prepared in just ten minutes or less!

Ingredients

6 **olives**
¼ oz. (7 g) **aged cheese** (sliced thinly)
10 **cherry tomatoes**
1 loaf **whole wheat crusty bread**

Makes: 2 servings
Calories: 104 calories per serving

Instructions

Slice the olives and tomatoes in half. Set aside.

Cut the crusty bread into bit-size pieces.

Slice the cheese thinly.

Combine all ingredients in a portable container.

3. Paprika Hard-Boiled Eggs

Paprika is a great ingredient to make hardboiled eggs more interesting and healthier at the same time.

Ingredients

1 tsp **paprika powder**
1 tsp **kosher salt**
2 tsp extra virgin **olive oil**
8 **hardboiled eggs** (sliced in half)

Makes: 8 servings
Calories: 85 per serving

Instructions

Slice the hardboiled eggs in half

Dip each half in extra virgin olive oil.

Sprinkle with a bit of paprika powder and kosher salt.

Serve immediately.

Enjoy during snack time!

4. Lemon Cream with Berries

Combining reduced-fat cream cheese with Greek yogurt creates a delicious mixture. Top it with berries of your choice. I recommend raspberries or blueberries for this.

Ingredients

2 cups **fresh berries** of your choice
2 tsp **lemon rind** (freshly grated)
1 tsp organic **honey**
3/4 cup plain **Greek yogurt** or low-fat **vanilla yogurt**
4 oz. (115 g) reduced-fat **cream cheese**

Makes: 4 servings
Calories: 151 per serving

Instructions

In a medium-sized bowl, break the cream cheese apart using a fork.

Add in the organic honey and the Greek yogurt or vanilla yogurt and beat everything together using a handheld electric mixer at high speed until the mixture is creamy and smooth. Stir in the freshly grated lemon rind.

Prepare 4 wine glasses or dessert dishes, and add a bit of lemon cream cheese mixture on each. Top with a layer of berries. Then, add another layer of lemon cream cheese mixture. Keep layering alternately until everything has been used up. Serve immediately.

You can cover the lemon cream cheese mixture and store it in the refrigerator for up to eight hours if you are not serving it immediately.

5. Fruit Couscous Salad

Couscous is a classic whole wheat dish usually served with meat, but is great with fruit salad too!

Ingredients

2 tbs **almonds** (toasted, chopped)
½ cup **raspberries**
½ cup **blueberries**
1 cup **nectarine** (chopped)
2 cups 100% **whole-wheat couscous** (cooked)
¼ tsp **ground black pepper**
¼ tsp **table salt**
2 tsp **shallots** (chopped)
1 tbs **apple cider vinegar**
2 tbs **orange juice**
2 tbs **extra virgin olive oil**

Makes: 4 servings
Calories: 244 per serving

Instructions

In a large mixing bowl, whisk together the apple cider vinegar, ground black pepper, table salt, shallots, orange juice, and extra virgin olive oil.

Add in the cooked couscous and stir well.

Add in the chopped toasted almonds, raspberries, blueberries, and the chopped nectarines. Toss gently until well combined.

Serve immediately.

6. Sautéed Carrot Salad

Eating carrots regularly can lower your blood pressure and cholesterol levels. They are a great ingredient and work well in salads. This one is quick and simple.

Ingredients

5-6 large **carrots**
2 **tomatoes** (sliced)
1 large **yellow onion**
2 tsp **olive oil** or **coconut oil**
1 pinch **salt** to taste (optional)

Makes: 2 servings
Calories: 85 per serving

Instructions

Wash and cut the carrots into julienne strips. Slice onion into thin rings, then also slice the tomatoes

Heat the oil of your choice in a frying pan. Sauté the carrots, onions and tomatoes over high heat until the onions are tender and browned.

Optionally, add salt to taste before serving.

7. Tzatziki

Tzatziki is a classic Greek specialty, a sauce with cucumbers, lemon juice, garlic, yoghurt, and dill that can accompany a wide variety of meals. It works very well on warm pita bread and with meat.

Ingredients

1 cup **Greek Yogurt**
½ **garlic** clove (minced)
½ large **cucumber** (peeled, halved lengthwise)
1 tbs fresh **lemon juice**
2 tbs **dill** (chopped)
Salt and **pepper** (ground)

Makes 3 servings
Calories: 135 per serving

Instructions

Simply combine the ingredients in a bowl. Season with salt and pepper, then add to it to other meals or use it on warm pita bread.

8. Shell Pasta Salad

Pasta salad with colorful Mediterranean ingredients is as much a meal as it is a treat.

Ingredients

1 lb. (450 g) **shell-shaped pasta**
4 oz. (115 g) **feta** (crumbled)
10 fresh **basil leaves**
1 cup sun-dried, oil-packed **tomatoes** (chopped)
½ cup **black** or **green olives**, (pitted, chopped)
½ cup **extra virgin olive oil**
¼ cup **red wine vinegar**
2 tbs **lemon juice**
Salt and **pepper**

Makes 8 servings
Calories: 345 per serving

Instructions

Cook the pasta according to packaging instructions, omitting salt and fat. Cook until it is tender, but not mushy. Drain and transfer to a bowl. Rinse under cold water, then drain again.

Add olives, tomatoes, and feta. Stir in the vinegar, extra virgin olive oil, and lemon juice. Add basil and season with salt and peppers, then toss to mix. Serve cold or at room temperature.

9. Orzo Pasta Salad

This is another Mediterranean pasta salad, using a rice shaped pasta called Orzo.

Ingredients

1 cup uncooked **orzo**
3 tbs pitted **kalamata olives** (chopped)
3 tbs **red onion** (chopped)
3 oz. **feta cheese** (crumbled)
6 oz. marinated **artichoke hearts** (chopped)
2 cups bagged **baby spinach** (chopped)
½ cup oil-packed, sun-dried **tomatoes** (chopped)
½ tsp **black pepper** (ground)
¼ tsp **salt**

Makes 12 servings
Calories: 215 per serving

Instructions

Cook the pasta according to packaging instructions, omitting salt and fat. Cook until it is tender, but not mushy. Drain and transfer to a bowl. Rinse under cold water, then drain again.

Add the olives, spinach, onion, feta cheese, tomatoes, and season with salt and pepper.

Drain and chop artichokes, reserving its marinade. Add both to the bowl.

Serve cold or at room temperature.

10. Roasted Potatoes

Roasted potatoes make a great snack and can also be used to accompany lunch or dinner. If you want to use big instead of small potatoes for this recipe, cut them into chunks.

Ingredients

3 lbs. (1.35 kg) small **Yukon potatoes** (peeled)
1 ½ tbs **butter** or **coconut butter**
3 tbs **extra virgin olive oil**
¼ cup **lemon juice**
4 tsp **thyme** (chopped)
¾ tsp **salt**
½ tsp **pepper**

Makes 7 servings
Calories: 225 per serving

Instructions

Preheat the oven to 400F (200°C).

Over medium heat, cook oil and butter in a pan for 4 minutes, or until the butter turns light brown. Stir constantly.

Remove from heat, then add potatoes and toss to coat. Transfer to a jelly-roll pan, spreading the potatoes in a single layer.

Bake for 45 minutes, or until potatoes are tender and turn light brown.

Transfer to a serving bowl. Add thyme, salt, pepper, and lemon juice, then toss to coat. Serve immediately.

Dinner Recipes

1. Mediterranean Nachos

Nachos are a simple yet flavorful dish. It is very easy to prepare and extremely satisfying. Though traditionally a Mexican dish, followers of the Mediterranean diet can still enjoy nachos by using this recipe.

Ingredients

Fresh **parsley leaves** (optional, chopped)
2 tbs **red onions** (minced)
¼ cup **tomatoes** (diced)
8 pitted **Kalamata olives** (sliced in half)
2 tbs **feta cheese** (grated)
2 tbs **hummus**
1 taco-sized **tortilla**
Extra virgin **olive oil** (for greasing)

Makes: 2 servings
Calories: 155 per serving

Instructions

Slice the flour tortilla into 8 equal wedge-shaped pieces.

Preheat the oven to 400 F (200 °C).

Grease a baking tray lightly with extra virgin olive oil.

Arrange the tortilla wedges onto the baking tray and brush the tops very lightly with more extra virgin olive oil.

Bake the tortilla wedges for 5 minutes, or until they are golden brown and slightly toasted.

Spread roughly half a tsp of hummus onto each nacho, then top with half a tsp of grated feta cheese.

Top all nachos equally with the minced red onions, diced tomatoes, and halved olives. Bake for another 5 minutes.

Sprinkle chopped fresh parsley leaves on top.

Serve immediately.

2. Barley and Eggplant Salad

This is a hearty dish with strong flavors. For vegetarians, the chicken broth can be replaced by water.

Ingredients

¼ tsp **cayenne pepper**
½ lb. (225 g) **pearl barley**
14 oz. (400 g) low-sodium **chicken broth**
¾ cup **water**
2 tbs **lemon juice** (freshly squeezed)
1 clove of **garlic** (minced)
1 cup fresh **parsley leaves** (chopped)
½ cup fresh **mint leaves** (chopped)
½ lb. (225 g) **cherry tomatoes** (quartered)
1/3 cup **olives** (sliced in half)
½ cup **red onions** (sliced)
½ tsp **coriander** (ground)
1 ½ tsp **cumin seeds**
1 cup **scallions** (chopped)
1 tsp **black pepper** (ground)
1 tsp **table salt**
10 tbs extra virgin **olive oil**
¾ lb. (340 g) **zucchini** (diced)
1 ½ lbs. (680 g) **eggplant** (diced)

Makes: 12 servings
Calories: 215 per serving

Instructions

Preheat the oven to 425°F (220°C). Place the oven racks in the lower and upper thirds of the oven.

In a large mixing bowl, combine the diced zucchini and eggplant and add in ¾ tsp ground black pepper, ¾ tsp table salt, and 5 tbs extra virgin olive oil. Mix well.

Divide the mixture into two greased baking trays. Roast the vegetable mixture in the preheated oven, with occasional stirring and switching the position of the baking trays halfway through the baking time, for about 25 minutes, or until the vegetables are tender and golden brown. Transfer all vegetables to just one baking tray, and reserve the other tray for later.

Heat 2 tbs of olive oil in a large pot, then add the cayenne pepper, ground coriander, cumin seeds, and chopped scallions. Stir well and cook for 1 minute. Add the pearl barley and cook for 2 more minutes with constant stirring.

Add the water and chicken broth and allow to boil. Once boiling, reduce to low heat and simmer for about 35 minutes, or until the barley is soft and all of the liquids have been absorbed.

Turn off the heat, cover and let it sit for 5 minutes. Transfer the cooked barley to the reserved baking tray and spread evenly to cover the bottom. Allow it to cool for about 20 minutes, or until it has reached room temperature.

To prepare the dressing, in a large mixing bowl, combine the remaining 3 tbs extra virgin olive oil, 1/4 tsp ground black pepper, 1/4 tsp table salt, minced garlic, and freshly squeezed lemon juice. Mix well until fully combined.

Add in the roasted vegetables, cooked barley, and the remaining ingredients to the dressing and toss well until fully combined. Serve immediately with slices of your choice of cheese.

Serve immediately.

3. Cherry Tomato, Garlic, and Eggplant Salad

This simple yet flavorful salad goes well with steak, lamb, or any Mediterranean meat main dish, but can be eaten and enjoyed on its own.

Ingredients

2 tbs **red wine vinegar**
2 tbs **dill** (chopped)
2 tbs **parsley leaves** (chopped)
¼ cup **onions** (chopped)
1 pint (530 g) **cherry tomatoes** (sliced in half)
6 cloves of **garlic** (peeled)
2 tbs **extra virgin olive oil**
1 ¼ lbs. (570 g) **eggplants** (peeled, sliced)

Makes: 4 servings
Calories: 135 per serving

Instructions

Preheat the oven to 350F (180°C). Arrange eggplant pieces in a roasting pan. Drizzle the extra virgin olive oil on top and toss lightly to coat the eggplant pieces. Roast in the preheated oven for 20 minutes.

Add in the peeled garlic cloves and continue roasting for an additional 25 minutes, or until the garlic and eggplant are soft. Once done roasting, allow it to cool for 10 minutes.

Chop the roasted garlic cloves finely, then transfer roasted eggplants and garlic to a large bowl.

Add the remaining ingredients into the eggplant and garlic mixture and stir well until fully combined. Add ground black pepper and table salt to taste. Allow it to cool to room temperature before serving.

4. Roasted Tomatoes and Broccoli

This recipe combines tomatoes, broccoli and olives into a delicious Mediterranean dish.

Ingredients

1 tsp dried **oregano**
¼ tsp **table salt**
10 pitted **black olives** (sliced in half)
1 tbs **lemon juice** (freshly squeezed)
½ tsp **lemon rind**
2 **garlic cloves** (minced)
1 tbs **extra virgin olive oil**
1 cup **grape tomatoes**
4 cups **broccoli crowns** (chopped)

Makes: 4 servings
Calories: 80 per serving

Instructions

Preheat the oven to 450F (230°C). In a large mixing bowl, combine the table salt, minced garlic, extra virgin olive oil, grape tomatoes, and chopped broccoli. Stir well to combine.

Spread evenly across a baking pan and bake for about 12 minutes, or until the broccoli just starts to brown.

While baking, mix together the dried oregano, halved olives, squeezed lemon juice, and grated lemon rind in a large mixing bowl. Add the baked vegetables and stir well until fully combined. Let it cool for a 5 minutes before serving.

5. Mediterranean Wrap

This recipe is a filling and delicious meal that takes only 5 minutes to make. These wraps are perfect for the Mediterranean diet and should get a spot in any meal plan.

Ingredients

1 tbs **vinaigrette**
1 ¼ tbs **basil leaves** (chopped)
2 tbs pitted **black olives** (sliced in half)
¼ cup **tomatoes** (chopped)
1/3 cup **feta cheese** (crumbled)
½ **avocado** (sliced, diced)
¾ cup fresh **baby spinach** (chopped)
1 9-inch (23 cm) **spinach wrap** or **tortilla wrap**
1 tbs regular **cream cheese**

Makes: 1 serving
Calories: 365 per serving

Instructions

Spread the cream cheese evenly on one side of the spinach or tortilla wrap. Add the cubed avocado, crumbled feta cheese, chopped basil leaves, chopped spinach, vinaigrette, and halved olives.

Roll up the wrap carefully and slice in half diagonally.

Serve immediately.

6. Paleo Slow Cooker Chicken

Mediterranean recipes are often dominated by ingredients such as lemon, olives and tomatoes. Serve this dish with mashed sweet potatoes.

Ingredients

1 **lemon**
¼ cup **olives**
15 oz. (425 g) **plum tomatoes** (roughly chopped)
¼ tsp **black pepper** (ground)
¾ cup **onion** (chopped)
2 tbs **drained capers**
12 bone in **chicken thighs**
1 tbs **olive oil** or **coconut oil**
Rosemary (optional, chopped)
Fresh parsley (optional, chopped)

Makes 6 servings
Calories: 215 per serving

Instructions

Grate the lemon to get 1 tbs of zest. Also, squeeze the lemon to get 1 tbs of juice. Combine the zest and juice in a bowl. Cover and refrigerate. Combine the onion, lemon juice, olives, drained capers and plum tomatoes in a slow cooker. Season the chicken thighs with pepper.

Heat the oil of your choice in a pan over medium heat. Place the chicken thighs in a pan, then cook for 3 minutes on each side until brown. Add the chicken thighs to the slow cooker. Cook for 4 hours on medium heat until brown and tender.

Place the chicken on plates and stir in the lemon sauce. Garnish with desired amount of rosemary and parsley.

7. Italian Tomato Meatballs

Most meatballs combine pork, beef and veal. This recipe uses a lighter sauce to intensify the flavor without adding much on calories and fat.

Ingredients

1 **egg**
1 tsp **salt**
1 **small onion** (minced)
6 **garlic cloves** (minced)
1 lb. (450 g) **lean ground beef**
½ tbs **olive oil** or **coconut oil**
14 oz. (400 g) **dice tomatoes**
2 tsp **Italian seasoning**
1 **bay leaf**
1 **egg white**
¼ **parsley** (minced)
2 lb. (900 g) **chicken** or **turkey sausage**
28 oz. (800g) **tomatoes** (crushed)
1 tsp **red pepper flakes**
1 cup **chicken broth**

Makes 8 servings
Calories: 210 per serving

Instructions

Whisk the egg and egg white together in a bowl. Add the parsley, garlic cloves and ¼ of the onion.

Combine the beef and sausage and stir to mix.

Roll the mixture into balls. The mixture should be enough for 22-25 meatballs, depending on the size you make them. Add to a slow cooker.

Heat the oil of your choice in a pan over medium heat. Sauté the remaining ¾ of the onion for 5 minutes until fragrant and tender.

Add the red pepper flakes, Italian seasoning, and garlic. Stir for 30 seconds before adding the diced tomatoes, bay leaf, crushed tomatoes and chicken broth.

Pour the sauce over the meatballs in the slow cooker and cook for 6 hours in low heat.

8. Carrot Garlic Soup

This is a delicious and healthy slow cooker meal for the whole family.

Ingredients

2 lbs. (910 g) **carrots**
3 **garlic cloves** (finely chopped)
1 tsp **curry powder**
½ cup **sour cream** or **coconut cream**
8 oz. (225 g) **shrimps** (peeled, cooked)
6 **white and green scallions**
2 tbs **fresh ginger** (chopped)
2 ½ cups low sodium **chicken broth**
1 pinch **salt**
Cilantro to sprinkle (optional)

Makes 6 servings
Calories: 177 per serving

Instructions

Combine the scallions, ginger, curry powder, garlic and carrots in a slow cooker.

Add 2 cups of water, then bring to a boil. Cook for 7 to 8 hours in low heat until carrots are tender.

Remove from heat and allow it to cool slightly.

Puree the soup in batches, then return to the slow cooker.

Add the sour cream or coconut cream and season with salt until completely heated through.

Ladle the soup into bowls and top with optional cilantro.

9. Slow Cooker Zucchini Dish

This dish combines many flavors, ranging from the exotic quality of coconuts to the tanginess of herbs.

Ingredients

2 **zucchinis**
5 cups (1.2 liters) **chicken broth**
½ cup **shallots** (chopped)
1 tsp **oregano** (crushed, dried)
3 tbs **butter** or **coconut butter**
1 tbs **extra virgin olive oil**
1 **yellow sweet pepper** (chopped)
2 cups **rice**
3 **garlic cloves** (minced)
3 cups **mushrooms** (sliced)
Italian flat leaf parsley

Makes 12 servings
Calories: 215 per serving

Instructions

Lightly coat a slow cooker with olive oil or cooking spray.

Add the zucchini, rice, oregano, salt and pepper, chicken broth, garlic, and shallots. Cover and cook for 4 hours in high heat.

Add the butter, then remove from heat. Set aside for 15 minutes. Pour in the vegetable broth, if the dish is too dry.

Heat the oil of your choice in a pan. Cook the sliced mushrooms, then transfer to plate.

Top with sweet pepper and parsley.

10. Lamb Chops in Greek Sauce

This recipes gives lamb a Greek touch, using a minty sauce. Alternatively, you can use Tzatziki for this.

Ingredients

8 4 oz. (115 g) **lamb loin chops** (trimmed)
½ cup **Greek yogurt**
2 tsp **oregano** (chopped)
3 **garlic** cloves (minced)
2 tsp **extra virgin olive oil**
1 tbs **mint** (chopped)
2 ½ tbs **lemon juice**
¼ tsp **sea salt**
¼ tsp **black pepper** (ground)

Makes 4 servings
Calories: 325 per serving

Instructions

Combine 2 tbs lemon juice, oregano, and garlic in a bowl.

Season lamb chops with salt and pepper, then coat with the mixture from the bowl.

Heat the olive oil in a pan over high heat. Add lamb chops and cook for 3-4 minutes on each side, or until desired level of doneness.

Remove from heat and allow to cool for 5 minutes.

Force the serve, combine yogurt, mint, and the remaining ½ tbs lemon juice in a bowl. Alternatively, use Tzatziki. Serve sauce with the lamb.

6871003R00043

Printed in Great Britain
by Amazon.co.uk, Ltd.,
Marston Gate.